ARMOR & ORNAMENT

Christopher Lee Miles

University of Alaska Press

Text © 2019 University of Alaska Press

Published by
University of Alaska Press
P.O. Box 756240
Fairbanks, AK 99775-6240

Cover and interior design by 590 Design.
Cover design by Madara Mason.

Cover art: *The Triumphal Chariot of Maximilian I (The Great Triumphal Car)*, Albrecht Dürer.
Photograph of a 1522 woodcut. https://www.metmuseum.org/art/collection/search/359787

Library of Congress Cataloging in Publication Data

Names: Miles, Christopher Lee, author.
Title: Armor & Ornament / by Christopher Lee Miles.
Other titles: Armor and Ornament
Description: Fairbanks, AK : University of Alaska Press, 2019. | Includes
    bibliographical references. |
Identifiers: LCCN 2018061122 (print) | LCCN 2019000772 (e-book) | ISBN
    9781602233881 (e-book) | ISBN 9781602233874 (pbk.)
Classification: LCC PS3613.I524 (e-book) | LCC PS3613.I524 A6 2019 (print) |
    DDC 811/.6dc23
LC record available at https://lccn.loc.gov/2018061122

FIRST OFFSET PRINTING

In Memory of
Michael Manly Miles
9-3-1983 to 3-9-2011

If then our faith we for our guide admit,
Vain is that farther search of human wit;
As, when the building gains a surer stay,
We take the unuseful scaffolding away.
Reason by sense no more can understand;
The game is played into another hand.
—John Dryden, "The Hind and the Panther"

His house of holy cards had collapsed
through his own ineptitude.
—William Trevor, *The Children of Dynmouth*

Contents

THREE

ONE

Is This Not a Strange Life to Which I Call You

i. m. Colleen Brownlow

Desiring the water of Communion,
the rootstock of the vine, the body
my body becomes when I enter
the vole's dream, that tunnel under sleep.

The throat to which this mouth leads
leads to the fear of what I desire.
This is called *faith*; it is also called *doubt*:
both teach my hands to travel

the soul's chiasmus, its fleshlooped wire.
Like all your gifts, these are clues.
In the course of play, I find a way
beyond the mirror: stop imitating,

stop stopping,
start digging through the wall
and spreading my net and drawing
my sword and smoking its blade

with the blood of my enemies.
The space you give me.
All my selves and the doors between them.
My movement in submersion

results in every shape on the surface:
outbreaks of violence, a virus

in the cell of every host.
I am still drawing you into this cavity.

What cavity, you ask.
From where you stand, I appear
to be singing, or maybe shouting.
I'm not. I haven't even breathed.

A Flaming Sword

i. m. Manly Miles

When days are dead hollyhock stalks.
When deer hides hang from the clothesline.
When frost salts the shingles
and ashes pepper the grass
and sparrows dive into the underworld
and return with beaks bristling with straw.
You rise from the gutter,
step through a widow spider's web,
fly to the field, and knife the corn.
Gnats and tassels haloing your head,
you harvest a scarecrow's silhouette,
a hybrid of man and god. The sun teeming
in the eyelets of your boots.
Communing with your failure
to commune, winnowing the Word
to a field of stubble, you rest beside the son
you made prodigal, feed branches
to the blazing feed bags. The radiance
warms us through our overalls.
Out beyond the outbuilding
the caustic plains, cauterized by erosion,
skewered by windmills. By removing fence lines
and plowing waterways, we welcomed
an unwelcome flood. The horizon a brim,
a flame spiraling your angel's blade.

The Storm on the Lake

Field, on whose back the tortuous corn grows.
Creeks and gravel pits, ditches lined with honeysuckle.
Lilies pinnacled at the mouth of a culvert, guarding

their pool of the sun's gold, waves of light revolving
like turrets, waves of prayer we are drowning in,
the sea's tongue cleaning the shores of our body.

So we're sailors, swimming and at the same time
drowning; shuffling ships, stacking decks.
But which card will help us measure the tale
of this flood, the flexible story of dragging
our feet across water, sinking like Peter when we doubt.

Holy Water in a Dry-House

i. m. William & Meda McCloud

This land a remnant, a lament
powered by nostalgia, a page
on which your wrath is written:
fire feeding on a collapsed barn.

We develop in history's placenta,
drink its mother's blood.
When a year of the war is over,
the children raise it to the sun,

a token to make one revolution.
I speak the Word with derision and slip
back into the armor that prevents light,
at certain angles, from entering my vision.

I have not gone from you.
Do not believe me when I say,
"I can wear whatever I want because
the body is a rack for hanging fabric."

The shades shook like mountains,
shuffling their order, breathing
through the straws of myth.
I saw all the dead

orbit the living through language:
the awe in Yahweh, the shank of ice
in Christ, the motion your fist
makes when you twist it in the air.

The Dynamited Mass

i. m. Mel & Bun Iverson

The molars in the mouth
of the prairie are nude
gravestones dressed in chaff,
embers on a hissing tongue.

We destroy the foundation
and bless the rubble.
We ply the nails from the boards
and set them on the anvil

and beat them straight
and hammer them in again.
The idea of origin, of source.
In this brief period,

this complex sentence,
this succession of clauses
that seems to rise, to climb,
we do not reach for the hand

that is held out to us;
we lift permed lengths of rebar
from the debris of the dynamited
Mass, raise and wave our kinked

crosspieces, straighten our arms.
Belief is a form of water:
we pour it into each pose we strike,
each pitch we throw.

Cain the Earthmover

An agrarian comfort doll to bind in plastic
and bury for drainage, a standard procession,
the absence of law. Like any average male,

I balance my lust with my vanity,
my vanity with my father's name,
which assures me I am a gun for history to fire,

a record of force, a death for the emperor
of life. Fog, closing in from the edge of a distance;
or distance itself, becoming fog.

Cultivated by sleep, governed by its furrow,
its sulcus. Because what I am is
I celebrate war's

dense colors: gray of granite, cream of silica.
There is nothing that cannot be made natural.
There is nothing natural that cannot be lost.

A bulldozer cleaving a treeless pasture,
its blade finessing stone, shaping garlands
of clay, spooling soil, churling earth.

To Rain

Who if not you will teach me how to lie
down, drink from the puddles into which you fell,
suck a pure vitamin from the polluted well,

let satisfaction cloud out my cry?
After you vanish, I see sugared mud,
a damp dimple, small veins in the earth's face,

narrow channels where your coursings erased
the rose pollen with a twisting of suds.
As I am this forked and earthbound creature,

so you, without wings, without limbs to move,
are left to the whim of the wind's maneuver;
and gravity, you are cupped in its curve.

Of your existence, I am never sure.
Distinct from, then joined with, other moistures,
you are the drenched sinew of my dry nerve.

My Scallop-Shell of Quiet

Thought's vegetation, the vista
for myself, a moment with the plain,
with what is plain, which isn't much,
but a grass veil, a plinth of bone.
I heard a chink when the elbow
of the pipe struck the skull
of the rabid fox. You gave me
the freedom to end its freedom;
poured it into me, pit and snare.
The destroyer to be called
by a tribunal of ravens; owls holding
court with visions; goatdemons
charging hedges, subdued
by the price of their own assault.

The Burden of the Valley of Vision

—Isaiah 22:1

If we do not watch all that goes by, or if we do,
it still goes by. Wetlands are their own vision:
the heron's legs nailing the scumpond,
the twitching moss, the marsh marigold.

Sometimes you see it on a predator's face:
weariness, not from having to kill,
but from having to put in so much effort
to kill. With practice, we acquire knowledge

of the wound that preceded our wounding.
We open doors, but the rooms we reach
are not garlanded. We roll down the windows
of our belief, tell stories about prophets

who tell stories, a picture of a picture. To walk
out of the trap, approach through comparison,
compare the marsh to the desert, come near
enough to say, "It was like this. This right here."

Burn Pit

In this burn pit of blownoff limbs,
we will never lose you, never find you.
Sitting in the pew, watching stained glass
parrot the light, each element a feather.

You hand me the calix, a vehicle
of blood. The nails that fix
your wisdom to the cross
bind me to the bread of your body.

We fashioned war, and war fashioned my defeat:
paths of the destroyer, the vessel
whose keel splits the sea's artery, the brine
bleeding creosote, pickling carcasses.

The House of the Forest

—1 Kings 7:2

Hickory, ash, poplar: the way forward
is through whatever obstructs you.

Watch us enter the opening in the wall
and become a lie, a thread of experience.

All you need is one chip off the rock of truth,
and you can create a movement,

a development in the story of civilization.
The way forward is not like electing

the candidate you support.
It's like learning the names of the trees

you've always admired: basswood, elm, beech.
Labor is the passage from time to eternity,

the achievement of mystery, a revelation
like the seepage of alkaline waters.

Beneath its skin of lilies and scum,
a pain leading to the cessation of pain,

years becoming days, days becoming shrines.
We make adjustments, tweak the law

to keep pollen coming through the window,
grains that we breathe, that fertilize our lungs.

A Procession in the Cave

The group we're listening to is made up of children
who believe they're adults. They believe this so fiercely
their bodies mature prematurely. By twenty years of age,

the vessels in their eyes have popped. They cry blood.
Their strategy is to take something we all experience
(such as dread, fear, or anxiety) and claim

they are the only ones experiencing it, the only ones
who *can* experience it. They build walls out of thoughts
and spy on us through the holes we drill in the walls.

We drill these holes so they have fresh air and sunlight
and a view of the rain when it falls, but they interpret
our drilling as aggressive; they think we're malicious,

that we don't care about what they care about. They don't
realize our care is the same. We just call it something else.
They rarely come to our festivals. We never hear them sing.

When one of them dies, they throw the body over the wall,
and we undress it, clean it, burn it, bury the ashes, and at
the ceremony, we stand in a circle and join hands and say,

"One day, in the language of salt, the sea will record
its conquest of us, and the clouds will look down and read
how certain we were there was something between us."

The Spell of the Covenant

To witness a miracle, a vision not born
in the body; in its beam, we study the veil,
how flesh conceals, disguises a network
in which prey is snared. A luminous edge
believes we come from four sources,
that those sources come from one,
that that one grew from the droppings of goats.
Six hundred miles to the south stands a range
of mountains: peaks like molars, enamels
greased with ice. I do not envy their mouth.
Like the serpent, I beg for release, clutching
the bars of my cage. It's not an underworld
I descend to, but a flooding basement,
foaming with prayers that once fell as snow.

Holy Convocations

—Leviticus 23:2

Now the year. The cause of green castings,
common and unlocked, the wellfailed.
Each farm peeks through its halfopen eye,

claims an acre. Your god, the bass throb.
Bulls lumber uphill, calves suckle milk,
the heifers lie on frosted grass. I imagine,

cheerful but menaced, a fanfare for twilight.
This year we'll gather a rhythm's awkward riddle,
unroll the transcendent. I imagine

mystery reenacted in the undertow,
feeding both grape and grain. A requiem Mass
for the hogs. A slab of limestone

in the orchard. A boy jumping into the river.
The year of briar and buckthorn. The year
we sail toward heaven in our unmade beds.

Scandalized People, Meaning All of Us

Let speech be more precious than time.
We look like Abraham looking at Isaac.
Keeping the winter of the past awake
is one way to chill the future.
Communion is more dark season
than morning glare, more raven
than river. The worm an acrobat
of dirt, stillness the enemy of desire.
Your fable is why the word *dead*
sounds present tense: because *then*
is always *now*, and *now* is always
your Word emptying itself of the age
in which it is spoken. So a briar's antler
rakes your skull, gathers your victory.

The Riches of Darkness

The liquor of tongues turned to stone,
phrases of a blitzed landscape, knuckles of vines,
stems choking witness, a clotted testament.

We test the architecture of your tomb,
cross the field in which your cross is burning,
burn the sheets of the ghosts of race,

the arc of our orbit governed by insect stars,
bloodsuckers nailed to the beast of night.
We are the ship carving land, cleaving

the wrong element. To uncover what is lasting
in what is not, we whistle at the heads
of dandelions, watch the wind milk their seeds.

The motion melts our vision: the eye follows
a river of butter through the air, all the way
to the center of a sour winter, a cream-

colored lawn surrounded by curds of snow.
Our pits have lips, and when they aren't
gagging on scorched garbage, they speak of you.

To Serve Those Who Do Not Serve

Dentist of rhetoric
polishing the enamel of lies,
your power bores;
your tongue presses us
against your cheek.
It's not flavor you're devoted to

but vertebrae,
how bones grow together,
come apart like Legos.
You shift gears
without changing speed,
dance without moving,

move without being seen,
arrive by departing.
You gift us the loaf
of the bread of healing,
crust over the wound,
both servants of your alchemy.

Bell-Sound

The quality of doubt, the conditions of belief,
the voice of one who hears the voice of God.

Not silence—soundless pageantry. As many gods
as persons claiming to represent those gods.

If voices and bodies are interchangeable,
we must be inside a myth. A second definition

of the noun *priest*: a mallet used to kill fish.
Visions pass, or are misremembered.

Armor becomes ornament, wood becomes wire.
You prefer a slice to the loaf, your lover

to the crowd. In the valley of speech. In the vision
of that valley. The fable in which that vision occurs.

The anvil resting on the altar. The spell passing
through parrotcolored glass, touching the spine

of the book in which I read of God's javelin,
an annunciation, wide as a feather, narrow as a nest.

TWO

The Thin Harvest

How they clothe us, wear us, the days of grain,
the days of stalks cracked to flat ocher strips,
the days of chaff, and silk, and kernels dented
at the crown, as if scooping out a kingdom
for cocoons, or the pearled eggs of spiders.
The days of soybeans between teeth; they taste
of tobacco, bitter goosefoot, wild garlic.
A combine of days, helmed in holy fire.
A cremation of homelands, the scorching
of what is sacred, the slowfalling estates
rising in ash, the ashes falling, pouring.
Un-understandable. Dawn wrecking into day,
night crashing into dawn, a terrible wonder,
a wonderful terror. I have felt them as
the washedout field feels the rain fill its ravine.
I have watched their wide hands loosen the wind,
or toss the dice of dark clouds. With what rage,
what boyish rage, I launch my tremoring
no at them. I, who accuse them of lacking
purpose, would, without them, be purposeless.

Sworn to Secrecy the Morning
He Performed the Sacrament

Rebuilding every delusion you destroy, a bloodless
bloodletting. Whatever word conceals our gestures,
uncover it. Read our blames and accusations,
the entire scandal. Snared in the traps
we set for our enemies, not knowing that's who we are.
That we design our wounds like kingdoms
so we can wander around inside them.
The beauty of landscape is the trauma it causes
to our idea of it. The beauty of trauma
is that it exchanges bodies for ghosts who wander the garden,
brushing ants from the peonies with brass combs.
We wonder if we should help them, or hand them scissors,
or shampoo, or fertilizer. "They're not hair," we say.
To which the ghosts reply, "We know."

Apron of Leaves

When you have nothing to bear
you will feel no weight

rise to illusion
unweighted by mercy or grace

cry for gold
though autumn glows its mineral

yellow leaves
all the coins have been tossed

landing
at the end of every branch

they will fall again
rot into a kind of slime

and you can wipe that across
your cheeks for memory

The Supernumerary
Persons Being Enrichers
of His Inheritance

The icicles of ash, the flames of snow.
The grain of memory, which is wood.
Tongues arranged in the pattern
of devotion, muscles of praise

teaching us song; the song ushering us
to our seats in the theater of power,
congealing the night sky into a pool
on whose surface our delusion

is reflected. Our knees
have lips. To genuflect is to kiss
the element out of which we grow.
Grinding alchemy's medieval salt,
we touch your covenant; we read
your grammar with our blind mouths.

Holy Convocations

—Leviticus 23:2

A chalky spell cast on the body
of your seasons, winter,
an arm whose hand is summer.
That's how you reach us.
That's how dawn dresses in robes

and dances. The freedom
of obeying depends on how well
you internalize the rules.
Nothingness permits one thing:
that we ask questions of it.

They can't be answered.
What matters is how we pose them,
what effect their posing has,
and which false answers we believe are true.
You asked me to find the Word;

to serve many things,
or to serve one thing well—
but all I've found are letters,
characters in a dream,
out of time and back again,

the body in which I float, the names
of those who are bound, prayer
and pageantry. The wind a nucleus
of light, the light a wind of cells:
I misspell you once again.

The Exasperated Spirit

Birches swooping into the fevered silence
of fortyfive below; hoarfrost hugging
the spruce boughs; silvered reflections,
octaves of the Pentecost. To be mouthless,
and to say too much. The oil of vanity
transudes repression's screen, glides
down the arm, reaches the fingers,
sweats through the skin, inking the page
with forms of nothing. Lost in the haunt
and hover of ice fog; exhaustion induced
by exhaust. The fable of Saint Lawrence
strapped to the grill; his flesh smoking
in the forest of traffic, the roadway of wood.
We may be refined, but only in fire.

Spun Wisdom

You realize the thoughts you keep having aren't thoughts.
They're sounds. There's a man in your head. He's dancing.
And the sounds are his boots hitting the floor of your mind.

It's a wooden floor. Looks like maple. But you hear no music.
What is he dancing to then? Does this man in your mind
have a man in his mind, and is it he who is making the music?

Or is it a woman? And if it were, would her music be different
from the man's because she once knew him, when she was
younger, when they were lovers? Or maybe they were

brother and sister, and they fell in love with the same man,
and this same-man rented porta potties and hauled them
to and from his customers behind a one-ton dually truck.

I could use a truck like that, you think. But you're overtaken
by the sound again. Only this time you don't hear it.
You see it. In black letters on the ceiling. They appear

to be cut from tissue paper. Now things are coming right.
You return to misinterpreting the sound as thought.
You relax. To celebrate your relief, you open the window.

You hear the crash of aluminum. It's the goats, banging
the lid of their watering tank. In the morning, you will feed them
ground corn. In the morning, they will eat from your hand.

The Blood Forsakes My Face

Learn to align your will with your wonder,
and chaos will never be sacrificed, not in this circus,
where your performance is judged by people

who are spokes in a wheel of suspicion.
They said the denier has become everyone
he wanted to be: a clown, a hyena,

a giant hawk-eyed angel wielding a hoary weapon.
My resolution: to no longer resolve: to accept
every wound spilling wonder. Walk between

the creatures whose shadows see through
me. If you reenter the garden, you must leave again.
Return to the war on the evening before battle

and embrace the fear that will be horror
in the morning. In Book Seventeen, Hector dons
the armor of Achilles: that is, a doomed man wears

the costume of another doomed man. If you murder,
be prepared for ghosts. Thorns in the blood. Worms
in the roses that are blooming in the womb of chaos.

The Stench of Cursed Ground

Flesh as the source of conversion,
the cell as translator:
from the language of experience
into the experience of language.

What Christ said,
and what he was said to have said,
the speech and the writing,
the eyeless dead

who live in the valley of vision
and sing of God's mountain.
You say I can't say that.
Explanations are cards:

even as a deck they're nothing
compared to night's backgammon sky,
twilight numbered by dice,
the iron we mistake for air.

You whose courage is cowardice,
whose role is a heap of ruins,
when you burn my house in the forest,
my mind is a sheet of ice,

a pond where I ponder.
With the beveled edge
of my prayer I chisel not knowing
from knowing nothing.

Holy Convocations

—Leviticus 23:2

To know you exist within the fable
of existence. To fable your knowing.
Because I seek you, I cannot know you.
For enmity is a bruise in our heads.
Grammar meaning enchantment,
meaning magic means the land of void
and vision is a page in the book of fables.
Your truth is an act, or it is nothing.
Because I cannot know you, I seek you.
I test my fervor for the serpent,
pretend to know the formless whole
from which we are formed, end up
like Samson, grinding grain in prison,
embracing what can't be touched.

Our Days All Pass
Awaiting Its Return

We mistake the dead for whatever
we're searching for: each other,
the source of metaphor,
a metaphor for the source of why

we search for anything at all.
Having constructed an inner room,
I'll be your splinter, a fragment
of the cup you will break.

To confront the excellences
of autumn, the claws of frost
pinching the boughs, cradling
the dead leaves, crawling the earth

at a crab's pace. Ornament
dissolving in the water of desire,
silence sugaring your grace.
A train lugging faith

to a station of the cross.
Keep me from the mimes
and their media, grasshoppers
of culture leaping screen-to-screen

in the weedy field. I am your glass.
You may fill me. You may pour out
the nothing I contain.

He Houghed Their Horses, and Burnt Their Chariots with Fire
—*Joshua 11:9*

blinded by the change
from worship to warship
watched it happen in a future
that hasn't happened
ride like a prisoner
on the bus of my trauma
down a furrow in the field of time
distracted by the need to see
someplace farther than where I am
it might be different
and if it isn't
it will have been worth
the cost of the journey because
denying you has no price
if the life it costs
is lost to death

They Held to Sanity So Hard They Were Insane

It's best to mock the age for what it was:
an experiment, a mistake we needed to make.
This not only keeps it at a distance,
it keeps that distance far from us,
where it belongs. If it comes too close
we go mad, creating options and features,
reasons to forget that our time here,
though brief, is worth more than anything
we've invented. But you can't blame
anybody for that: the people had been seeking
joy, and they found it where they always do,
in mischief, and maybe that had something
to do with the caves: after years of yielding
nothing, they finally yawned and gave us
a good look at their wisdom teeth.
We liked giving consideration to something
that did not require it, but we did not like
being dragged into the earth, and our resistance
to it grew into a political movement,
though some called it a monument,
and claimed it had been there for years.
There was good in this, though by now the good
was halfbaked, nothing but a saccharine dough.
More recently, we've been driving out
to the gravel pits and combing the moss
growing on the rotting logs that line the shore.
They were once majestic elms, bristles
growing up through flesh of the earth,
and brushing their hair with metal rakes
is a peaceful way to praise their death.

The Burden of the Valley of Vision
—Isaiah 22:1

As long as there are cellos with wings,
as long as there are notes in the ritual
of your history, the flood will teach us
thirst, the drought will teach us drink.

Between you and us, between the pages
in the books of Hebrew, between
you and our wish to measure you:
a thornwired skull, a circle of allegories,

an unassailable boundary. We fall,
are inclined to the horizon, to what
the horizon holds, radiation available
to our senses: we sense you radiate.

We carry the crux, the casual arrival
of cancer, sealing its rupture around
our ruptured lives, bands of illness
binding us to death, tumors seeking

a sacred interpretation, a dread
that summons grace. "Look up,"
we say, as if to see who could help,
as if who could help could be seen.

The Morning Light

A stalk of light that cracks the peony bud,
that green egg with a flower for a yolk.
Our hands, held open, reaching down to touch
what passes beneath the course of knowledge.

We don't know what we're looking for. If we did,
we wouldn't look. We wouldn't watch the film
of ourselves expending our spirits in a waste
of shame. Sex: almost like a field from which

we've been exiled. We reenter, feeling
at home in the desert of our bodies. The water
of the mirage anoints us, an extreme unction.
Meanwhile, our children glue two mornings together,

setting dawn's careful seal. We know we pray
because our prayers won't be answered.
Until we learn to read a reply within
the illusion that we are disillusioned.

Dawn's Careful Seal

With every quality of brilliance, and all the brilliance of darkness,
the Lord said, "Fill your mouth with your own feces,
squeeze it through your clenched teeth, and smile, my son."

I replied, "Do what you will. For what I do comes to nothing.
So I come to be named, to enter the grammar of your fable.
Because my movement is unceasing, I assume

I leave something behind: a trail, a trace, an impression.
It feels that way, but it isn't true. The motion
is more side-to-side than ahead or reverse, more lateral

than literal, though the professors claim everything
is a metaphor, which means this crab-walk is a disease
I won't be able to cure until I'm motionless. But I'm not tired yet.

I'm going to stay up and watch the butchers behead
the angels. It'll remind me of language, of wandering,
of wandering through language, which is like wind

you can see with your eyes closed. Being displeased
with any circumstance cannot be prevented, but if you
can get rid of it in the course of play, no penalty remains."

Air Craft

Out of manurecarpeted pastures,
out of the soup of rotting soybeans,
your claim is blooming, a jet breaking

the sound barrier, a supersonic flower.
Some say you are a symbol of freedom;
others say you are the vehicle of death.

They lack agreement. Our voices
are wind. Our arguments are formed
by torsion, twisted thought. Our evil

is evergreen; days minted with murder;
nights the herb of violence has flavored.
If the clown is our boss, if the warrior

is also the clown, then who conducts
the joys that can't be ordered on Amazon,
that can't be clearcut from the jungle.

When the wind twirls its music,
and the dust dances, we rehearse you.
When the wind spins the tongue-leaves

of the elm, we rehearse you. When
the inkcolored squidcloud extends
the tentacle of its tornado, we rehearse you.

THREE

Bodies into Hills, Hills into Homes

We take our time so you can give us time
to take our hymn to the mountain called Ester.
On its south face, a chute where ravens
carry us messages from the dead. We never
understand them, but we understand our
misunderstanding. The trail there is a scar;
our feet won't let it heal; it bleeds schist, roots.
The moose have paths that cross our own.
Love is many things but mainly an exercise
in learning not to corral your confessions like horses.
They're too muscled to be sealed in words;
they buck against it; they want to become
movement, to refuse to measure what it feels like
to be here or there because we aren't anywhere
if not with the gods whose deaths allow us
to hear what the dead are saying: "Because you
misunderstand our singular meaning,
the only meaning we ever had, you don't believe
there is one. Instead, you believe in what
you've been given: all the time it takes
to take your hymn to the mountain called Ester."

Thinking Is Weeping Entering Eternity

Caught in your net, yanked from my blue oblivion.
The cords in the message are the message.
Your garment fashioned from music.
The rhythm of your departure: that is to say,
of your affection. The dove's purr is only one
detail of devotion, of who Christ was,
and of who he was thought to be; the eyes
of the kestrel; the error in Eros; me, always losing
what I know and never knowing it. A small room,
about five by eight, where a monk may wash his feet.
All you reflect reflected back. Maybe
you sit on the liquid seat of magnetism.
Maybe you sickle the sedge in the ditch.
Maybe no one does. Maybe we all refuse.

On Ester Mountain

When I removed my armor, I became vulnerable.
There was no porcupine to bless the quills
I had been hiding. I was a prayer questing for an echo
in the well of God. Wanting to be needless,

needing to be wanted, I took desire by the hand,
as if to lead it. But I was led. I wore a lightemitting
suit of voltage, arms raised to the Lord of Hosts.
Faith was silent, but I knew it wanted

to tell me what the story told everyone else:
you can't be both pretentious and a fable.
You have to choose, and my choice was true,
so I called it an animal, leashed it to the stump,

and fed it hotdogs. When the flowers I never picked
turned to the light I never reached for,
my disappointment was insulation,
preventing loss of pain, intrusion of danger.

I was imitating the imitations of others,
recalling my days as a thief, my doubletongue,
my shock on the seat of mercy. I understood
that we all must serve; that even if we turn

our bodies into hills, and those hills into homes,
the river will still flood those homes,
and the rain that will still fill that river
will still bring down the sky when it falls.

An Orgy of Absence

To fuck for money. To adorn the genitals
with silk. To stop identifying ourselves
with nations and face the same problems
we faced before nations existed.
To prostitute power, make comfort
our pimp. Or not. In which case a new deal.
A new distribution of value. The goal
of globalism is to build an engine
whose rotary force is powerful enough
to suck all existing matter into a single point
and create another big bang. Our wish
for destruction. Actually a wish to be
forgiven. When you have nothing to bear.
You will feel weightless. You will not
touch. Or be touched. You will not.

To Take Corporeal Shape

To see such thrust, such lift alofting house-lids
and heifers, pickup trucks and telephone poles:
all blown in the hazegray skygyre. To see each

plucked, pancaked, and sliversplit structure;
each vacuumedclean machine shed: tractors
wrenched and gripped by windforce, pitched

past the State Line Road, into the marsh. Then,
to see that sunflower, its yellow fruiting head,
unscathed in the heart of a stormclawed field.

The Morning Light

I begin as the day begins, like a vision of itself,
the rye of morning, graincolored light wiping
the loafshaped pig shed on the horizon.

Your buried martyrs in the sky, the marrow
of your boneless supplicants. To neutralize,
make free or clear. I was ready to receive your psalm,

but the night was a hand that refused to open.
Much of it did not lie in the truth, but it was truthful,
as was superstition, the presence of what was

no longer present, bees scrabbling the clovers,
the field so wet we called it alligator acres,
and the one beside it nothing but sand knobs.

Who Christ was, who he was said to be,
versions cast and forged, ironed into language.
It is one thing to imagine you, another to be

imagined by you, or by what I think of as you.
The dead, who know their calling,
are not ghosts, and the ghosts,

who don't know their calling, are not dead.
A serpent's path from the grass to the tree,
from the tree to a tunnel under the fortress

of ignorance, the movement an alphabeting,
a glyphing among flecks of minerals,
explosives waiting for their sharp release.

Dining at the Core of an Old Silence

Wasps of need, the sting of needless pleasures,
insects of instinct, nests in our flesh.
Your roots growing down from the sky.

The elm stump. Your rib rubbing my throat.
The young lion and the aging serpent.
So I began to read the Gospel of John.

It was difficult for me to understand it.
When I began to understand it was because
I had been glad to discover in certain passages

your image. I attended to that image
as to a place. I drew a map of that place.
And that map led me to give you all I had not

given myself. Yet, here it is. Honey cupped
in each cell, golden blood on the thistle crown,
a path perceived, a compass of wood.

The Soul's Chiasmus

Parallels between the aurora and compassion:
both are pitiless, unmeasured, unwilling
to descend and look you in the eye.
So knowledge poisons fable, the reality
we've wrapped ourselves in. The maestros
of history render each event palatable
to the human intellect. The days are a ridge
of land. The political sphere becomes a receptacle
for acid, a battery, its wires twisted to meet
the twists in perception, a wicked prejudice.
The residue of kenosis. Sea lice clinging
to the halibut's skin. The disgusting elegance
of celebrities, polished narcissism,
chrome on the media's vehicle.
Tenor: when you release the prisoner,
the dark self you've locked in your ribcage,
you murmur and mutter about the lack
of company. "There's more than enough light,"
you say, "but no one to share it with."

A Crown of Thistles

The trick of pain is to appear permanent.
For a moment, it compresses eternity,
makes a wedge of time and jams it in our jaw.
In the lesions, you smear the sugar of wonder.
You shaped the pain that shapes us:
to reach this beach, we had to sacrifice
every third child to the god heroin.
Every mother who refused to give birth
after her second—there were many
though we warned them that if they had one,
they had to have three—was flailed
with a rope until her back was a map:
valleys of torn flesh, creeks of blood,
lakes of blisters. On the other side
of those mountains, we will build our theater
of power. The ghosts of the sacrificed
will be the jesters who command our stage.
Their mouths will wake us to their haunting,
and we'll want to know what that means.

A Detail of Devotion

Like shades at a festival of light
we wonder why the wound won't heal,
why we even want to know why
the wound won't heal, why there's

a wound at all, why not no wound.
Because the formula for war is inexact,
once it has been calculated,
the air becomes oblique, spread out before us.

Hungry ghosts arrive, so-called sacred men,
the cults of luxury and of usury.
We lay eggs, inside of which grow
embryos of malice, the yolk

of every soldier's shellshock.
We clip the wings of certain birds,
fashion nests for our inheritance,
the flight we dread, that we were born for.

A Cipher for the Symbol of Zero

A worm in my blood, a rose in my worm,
a sense of infinity, the idea that every room
should be composed like a painting of a room.
The power to make pity fade without a poppy.

The grooves along which the cranes glide.
Whatever lands here, we hold it. We're the guest,
the message in an age of mess. Each cross
displays a creature, each creature is crucified

in the shade of your tower. Your trusses,
struts, and skids. Cherrypicked passages
from Leviticus. One moment we're killing each other,
the next we're weaponless, loving our enemies.

So there must be a fulcrum, a stable
where horses are kept; a small room, unadorned,
where a monk may wash his feet. I study my map
in the morning, before geography dawns.

Like a monk would, I tell myself, but I leave
my solitude, thread myself into the sky's abacus,
certain only of my servitude, that I'm a member
of this mob, this god who believes it is a beast.

Choke the Word

—Mark 4:19

Clean as combustion, as soot, the fulltime
anger squadron, their misanthropic machine.
I wish to enjoy the company of people
who do not enjoy the company of other people.
The ink scored into the sheetrock above the urinal
demands I RAPE THE RAPE WHISTLE.

"Of course you do," the voice of the flushing says.
The speech of the water is a whirl, the motion
a hypnosis. When, after one post, there comes another,
and you notice long wires between them,
chances are you've arrived at a fence.
From the spine of the altar to the spell

of the covenant, about that far. Magic
making money of sex and laundry of money.
Fabric of lust purchased at the cost of balance.
The land of Canaan, and the Canaan of marriage.
Like a runner, I am governed by the pace I set,
not by the speed at which you demand I go.

Under What Shadow

Whatever is sold is tied to the spindle
of the spine, where the nerves all link
their needles, and the moons all bleed
their milk. Sleeping, I remember.
Falling, I do not. In the velocity of light,
I find judgment, fruit rusting on the vine.
To seek the umbilical is justified.
It may be sacred. If there is attendance.
If what is attended to in those moments
are those moments. I stay up all night,
trying not to try. The mind maneuvers
its scream into the hollows under the branches.
When fables exist as sound in the theater
of memory. *Invisible Solid*, it says on the
deodorant. The brand name is *Secret*.

The Grooves along Which the Cranes Glide

Regardless of your existence. Regardless of my own.
The turbine turns. You attain what you desire
and continue desiring. You believe you're directing your body,
but really you're being drawn to a world
of spinning blades, combustion, columns of water.

Like most ideas, the one we live in is beautiful
and insubstantial. If it were an instrument,
it would be a cello, not because it's made of wood
or has four strings, but because it rests on a metal spike.
The turbine turns, pressurizing air. A system of gearwheels

in which unnecessary sexual needs rotate more quickly
than the driving shaft of perception. I wonder
if we could ever remove our social beauty,
learn not to play the game in which we are imprisoned,
lower ourselves into the bucket seats, drive into the well.

Because we believe in water, we follow every lure
and call ourselves fish. You can be in an abyss
and not even know it. You can know it and not care.
You can welcome yourself to the arctic heat of home,
the bread burned by your belief in it.

Ornamental Armor

The thoughtless crowd throws stones of thought.
So I kneel, not to be knighted, but to be necklaced
with your yoke, the bridle of mystery, soul's crosspiece.
When the Lord said, "Eat your own shit," I replied,
"When your temple was destroyed, you survived ruin
because we carried your fragments into the desert."
Not all predators are demons, but every demon
derives its power from being perceived as a predator.
I did as I was commanded, but there was no manna.
Only pestilence, bitter arrows fastened to my tongue.
Secular trinity of our age: those who die at war,
those who give birth to the ideas we go to war for,
and those who come back from war with the idea
that those who died at war are living in the sky.

Armor & Ornament

Because the festival of unleavened bread
could not keep the unborn from the ovens,
or the ovens from burning, or the ashes
from being swept into the mouths of the forgetful,
or the forgetful from laying their disgust
at each other's feet, we were obsessed
with the pendulum of power, how it swayed
from asses to elephants, elephants to asses.
We designed logos so the light of desire
shined through a shape we understood.
The river knew our memories and mocked them
with its flowing. Phantom trees on the shore,
their ghost arms milking the spleens of demons.
Satan: eel-like, armored in his inviolable secret,
ornamented with scales and claws and spurs:
pissed his knowledge of salt into our mouths.
A serpent advertised apples with the promise
of paradise. But that's where we were. Still,
we chewed through the taste of his shadows,
were led into a forest of mirrors: each held up
by an ape refusing to watch the documentary
of our exile. Later, beneath a cleft oak,
we bound the lamb of our curse and cut its throat.

The Armor of Light

—Romans 13:12

The humming of those who strike from a height
at which nothing is sacred because everything is a target.
We won't hear or see until the queen is fertilized
with something more than meaningless talk.

Satellite eyes turning in sockets that are ditches
in Dante's pit. Speeches drop, and the applause is fire.
The witch requires no broom to sweep the sky.
She glides, ink through air, marking the missile's path

with the felt tip of her pointed cap. The diction
of her drone is distant, on the edge of something
we don't understand. We don't have to explain
the concept of truth anymore. It's not that we're all liars,

though we are. It's not that we can't conceive it
any other way, because we can. It's that
when we go to explain it a number of people
refuse to listen, which bothers us, so we stop talking

to them so we can talk to ourselves about why
they aren't listening, about what we're doing wrong,
and by this point we're lost, so enmeshed
in other considerations that the moment has passed.

Acknowledgments

Thanks to Madara Mason, Zoe & Finn Hill; William & Kay McCloud; William & Colette Miles; Elizabeth Miles & Ella Bridge; Tommy & Quinn Miles; Robert Brownlow; Nelson and Kay Miles; Jill Osier; G. C. Waldrep; Peggy Shumaker; Cody Kucker; Nate Bauer; Chris Lott; Joeth Zucco; Krista West; Susan Hauser; Lauren Cobb; Derick Burleson; Amber Flora Thomas; Mark Christensen.

Thanks to the editors of the publications in which the following poems first appeared, a few in earlier versions:

The Cincinnati Review: "Holy Water in a Dry-House"
concīs: "A Flaming Sword," "An Orgy of Absence"
The Cresset: "Bell-Sound"
Hampden-Sydney Poetry Review: "The Thin Harvest," "To Rain"
Laurel Review: "Spun Wisdom"
Poecology: "To Take Corporeal Shape"
River Styx: "The Armor of Light"
West Branch: "Holy Convocations" part 1

Notes

"Is This Not a Strange Life to Which I Call You"
The title is from Thomas Traherne's *Centuries, Poems, and Thanksgivings*, "The First Century," passage 45.

"Holy Water in a Dry-House"
The title is from *King Lear* 3.2.9 in *The Riverside Shakespeare*.

"Cain the Earthmover"
There is nothing that cannot be made natural. There is nothing natural that cannot be lost: see Blaise Pascal's *Pensées and Other Writings*, Oxford's World Classics, translated by Honor Levi, p. 124, entry 523: "Man's nature is: wholly nature. *Wholly animal*. There is nothing that cannot be made natural. There is nothing natural that cannot be lost."

"My Scallop-Shell of Quiet"
The title is from "The Passionate Man's Pilgrimage" by Sir Walter Raleigh.

"The Burden of the Valley of Vision"
This poem is for Suzanne Bloom and Drew Harrington.

"Scandalized People, Meaning All of Us"
The title is from "The Question of Anti-Semitism in the Gospels," in *The Girard Reader*, edited by James G. Williams, p. 215.

"The Riches of Darkness"
The title is from Traherne's *Centuries, Poems, and Thanksgivings*, "The First Century," passages 32 and 33.

"Bell-Sound"
priest: a mallet used to kill fish: from *Concise Oxford English Dictionary*, 2011.

wood becomes wire: from the song "Mercy Seat" by Nick Cave & The Bad Seeds: "In Heaven His throne is made of gold. . . . Down here it's made of wood and wire."

"The Thin Harvest"
The title is from "Rural Life" by George Crabbe.

"Sworn to Secrecy the Morning He Performed the Sacrament"
The title is from the song "Trinity," performed by Common Market.

"The Supernumerary Persons Being Enrichers of His Inheritance"
The title is from Traherne's *Centuries, Poems, and Thanksgivings*, "The First Century," passage 15.

"The Exasperated Spirit"
The title is from *Little Gidding* by T. S. Eliot.

"The Blood Forsakes My Face"
The title is from "Windsor Castle" by Henry Howard, Earl of Surrey.

a giant hawk-eyed angel wielding a hoary weapon: from "Parker's Back," a Flannery O'Connor short story, found in The Library of America's *Collected Works*, p. 656.

"Our Days All Pass Awaiting Its Return"
The title is from "How Hard Is It to Keep from Being King When It's in You and in the Situation" by Robert Frost.

"They Held to Sanity So Hard They Were Insane"
The title is from the short story "It Spoke of Exactly the Things" by Barry Hannah.

"Dawn's Careful Seal"
if you / can get rid of it in the course of play, no penalty remains: *Official Rules of Cards Games*, p. 60: "A player can not, however, be prevented from leading or playing a card liable to be called; if he can get rid of it in the course of play, no penalty remains."

"Thinking Is Weeping Entering Eternity"
The title is from the poem "A Gloss On *To the River*" by Tim Lilburn, found in his collection *Kill-Site*.

"An Orgy of Absence"
a new deal: *Official Rules of Card Games*, p. 61: "If either of the adversaries has more or less than his correct number [of cards], there must be a new deal."

"To Take Corporeal Shape"
The title is from section IX of *The Triumph of Love* by Geoffrey Hill.

"Dining at the Core of an Old Silence"
Geoffrey Hill again, this time *Ludo*, strophe 21.

"Armor & Ornament"
Satan . . . armored in his inviolable secret: from René Girard, *I See Satan Fall Like Lightning*, translated by James Williams, p. 187: "The secret of Satan is inviolable."